SOFTWARE EVALUA
A CRITERION-BASED
APPROACH

Ronald D. Owston
York University

Prentice-Hall Canada Inc., *Scarborough, Ontario*

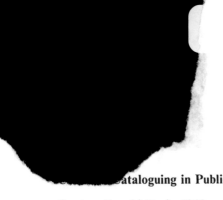

ataloguing in Publication Data

Owston, Ronald Davis, 1945-
Software evaluation

Bibliography: p.
ISBN 0-13-821620-7

1. Computer software - Evaluation. I. Title.

QA76.76.E93096 1986 005.3 C86-094420-4

Prentice-Hall Inc., Englewood Cliffs, *New Jersey*
Prentice-Hall International, Inc., *London*
Prentice-Hall of Australia, Pty., Ltd., *Sydney*
Prentice-Hall of India Pvt., Ltd., *New Delhi*
Prentice-Hall of Japan, Inc., *Tokyo*
Prentice-Hall of Southeast Asia (Pte.) Ltd., *Singapore*
Editora Prentice-Hall do Brasil Ltda., *Rio de Janeiro*
Prentice-Hall Hispanoamericana, S.A., *Mexico*

ISBN 0-13-821620-7

Production Editor: Jessica Pegis
Manufacturing Buyer: Matt Lumsdon

Printed and bound in Canada by Imprimerie Gagné

1 2 3 4 5 IG 91 90 89 88 87

Table of Contents

Preface

I first began to look seriously at the evaluation of microcomputer software at York University, when I became director of a cooperative project with IBM Canada Ltd. The project called for the evaluation of educational software and for the results to be entered into an on-line database available to educators across Canada and beyond.

This means of distributing the evaluations imposed certain constraints on the evaluation procedure. The resulting evaluations had to be concise—no more than a screenful of text; otherwise, they would be tedious to read. Brevity, however, could not be an excuse for lack of meaning and rigor.

The evaluations also had to be credible. Even though we intended to select only experienced teachers with solid pedagogical expertise to do the evaluations, their names might be unknown to database users on the other side of the country. Whatever evaluation procedure we used, we had to give database users some assurance that all evaluations were conducted using sound methodology and criteria.

Finally, the evaluations had to produce reliable results. One of the main functions of the database was to enable users who had read the evaluations in the database to choose a handful of appealing software packages for closer inspection. Therefore, the evaluation procedure had to allow different evaluators, using the same criteria, to come up with similar ratings of any given title. Without this kind of reliability, meaningful comparisons of software packages would be almost impossible to make.

I began searching the literature for a suitable evaluation procedure, and soon came to the conclusion that no published procedure would be entirely satisfactory. Moreover, I became somewhat dismayed at the lack of rigor evident in published evaluation techniques: educators were using evaluations done with such techniques to help them decide which software to buy and use. I had seen no published analyses of the validity or reliability of these approaches, or even any summary statistics to assist in their interpretation. The procedures also appeared to be developed in a void, without regard for the large volume of research that has been published during the past 25 years in program, curriculum, and school evaluation.

As a result, I set out to develop an evaluation approach that would both operate within the constraints of the database and take advantage of research in the field of evaluation. The approach that evolved was fundamentally different from earlier methods: it offered a global, or holistic, perspective of software. Evaluation would no longer be limited by checklists of isolated requirements. Instead, panels of teachers would rate the overall value of the software in several key areas using a criterion-based evaluation tool known as the *York Educational Software Evaluation Scales (YESES)*. Freed from the tyranny of checklists, panel members would be able to discuss such issues as the total impact the software has on the student or the value of the software in the classroom.

After refining panel evaluation for over two years and performing evaluations with several hundred teachers, I realize that the procedure provides an unexpected bonus: it forms the core of a valuable professional development activity for teachers. Now teachers can explore software with their colleagues; they can compare and contrast their ideas about software, learn how different developers approach software design, and discover the capabilities and limitations of the microcomputer.

The purpose of this book is to describe and explain this approach within the broader context of evaluation as a discipline. In Chapter 1 the reasons for evaluating software are given and the field of evaluation is discussed. An overview of existing evaluation techniques and their limitations is presented in Chapter 2. This overview serves as an introduction to Chapter 3, in which the panel evaluation process and YESES are described. Chapter 4, the final chapter, discusses what you should expect from a panel evaluation, and some of the potential problems of the procedure.

Many people shared their ideas in creating the evaluation procedure described in this book, perhaps none more than Hugh McCully of the Halton Board of Education, who was visiting associate professor at York University the year the project began. To him I would like to express my appreciation for his help and encouragement. I would also like to thank Andy Effrat, Dean of the Faculty of Education, for without his support this book would not have been written. The comments and suggestions of Laverne Smith and Frank McIntyre during the early stages of the design and try-out of the panel evaluation procedure were most valuable as well. Further, I am indebted to the many colleagues in my faculty and teachers who evaluated software using this procedure and gave helpful feedback. In particular, I would like to thank those whose evaluations appear in Appendix C: Claudette Antoine, Jerry Blair, Peter Board, Bev Bowen, Paul Davidson, Curt Dudley-Marling, Judy Goodman, Jane Gow, Barbara Komorowski, Cathy Kotsopoulos, Hugh McCully, Ray McDonnell, Ellen McGuire, Marywinn Milne, Lois Morancey, Gabrielle O'Reilly, Karen Scott, Dennis Searle, Margaret Sperling, Pauline Tetley, and Zatoon Vania. I owe a further debt of gratitude to IBM Canada Ltd. for their generous support of the cooperative project from which this book evolved.

I am appreciative to those involved in the planning and production of this book as well. Gary Bitter, Arizona State University, William G. Egnatoff, Queen's University, and John E. Walsh, University of Western Ontario reviewed the proposal for the book and willingly shared their experience and expertise to help guide its development. Thanks also to Patrick Ferrier, Jessica Pegis, Marta Tomins, and the staff at Prentice-Hall Canada for their enthusiasm and professionalism in turning an embryo idea into a finished product.

And finally, thanks to my wife Anke who has always been a source of support throughout my professional life.

Ronald D. Owston
York University

SOFTWARE EVALUATION:
A CRITERION-BASED
APPROACH

Chapter 1 Software Evaluation

Educators are forever evaluating. Teachers evaluate the progress of students, compare students' reactions to different teaching methods, and determine which teaching materials are the most effective. School consultants evaluate curriculum, decide which textbooks to recommend, and assess the value of different teaching strategies. Principals evaluate staff performance, look for ways to improve the organization of instruction, and compare different timetabling schemes. Supervisory officers monitor the performance of different schools, evaluate the effectiveness of new instructional programs, and seek cost effective ways of delivering existing programs and services. Now with the ever-increasing use of microcomputers in schools, educators have something else to evaluate—computer software. Why do we need to evaluate software? What can we learn from the general field of evaluation that can help us evaluate computer software? We will try to find answers to these two questions in this chapter.

Why Evaluate Software?

Surely we don't want to evaluate educational software just because we feel we should. There are enough chores involved in preparing for teaching and learning in school without this added task. So before we begin to evaluate software we must have a clear idea of the purpose of evaluation, know who is likely to use software evaluations, and understand the reasons why evaluation is necessary.

Purpose of Evaluation

The purpose of any evaluation is to increase understanding. For example, before buying a car we want to know more about the model we are considering. So we take the car for a test drive, read the manufacturer's brochures, speak to others who own the same model, and so on. What we are doing is increasing our understanding of the car to help us make a decision on buying it. Similarly, when we evaluate software we are saying that we want to understand the software better than we did before reading or doing an evaluation. We may want to learn about the software's goals and how effective it is in allowing users to accomplish them; we may want to find out about various technical features of the software; or we may want to determine the quality of the software's documentation. Our reasons for wanting to understand the software better may range from making a decision about using it in our own classes, to giving feedback to the software's developer for improving it.

Users of Evaluations

There are three groups of people who are likely to need the kinds of information about educational software that evaluations can provide—classroom teachers, school consultants or coordinators, and software developers. Many schools and school boards now have software libraries for teachers. Teachers may want to choose software from such libraries to use in their classrooms, but are not certain which packages would be most appropriate. This is an opportunity for teachers to do their own evaluations or read evaluations done by others. If there are many packages in the library that seem to be suitable, evaluations done by others would help in narrowing the choice to a few packages to be examined in greater detail. On the other hand, if there are not many alternatives in the library, teachers could evaluate each one before making a final selection. Teachers may also be asked to make recommendations for purchasing software. Here too evaluation would play an important role. Teachers might carry out evaluations themselves to make recommendations, or they may collect evaluations done by others to arrive at recommendations.

School consultants and subject area coordinators are another group that is likely to make use of evaluations. They too may be in a position to make recommendations for purchasing and using software; however, they are likely going to be selecting software from a much larger pool—perhaps all the software on the market for several grades and subject areas. In some cases, they could be selecting software for all grades and subjects taught in their school. Consultants and coordinators, therefore, are probably going to rely more upon outside evaluations than teachers would. Their task may be to sift out from the large number of possible packages available, a few that they will then examine more closely.

The third group that is likely to make use of evaluations is software developers. While the needs and uses of evaluations for the first two groups are somewhat similar, the third group's differ considerably. Developers look to evaluation as a way of improving their products. Poor evaluations would probably cause a publisher to improve or even discontinue a product. On the other hand, favorable evaluations may lead the publisher to develop new products having features similar to the original product. Most educators would agree that both of these results are desirable, assuming of course that the evaluations are fair.

Reasons for Evaluating Software

Now that we've looked at the purpose of software evaluation and its potential users, we can list some reasons why software should be evaluated.

Software Quality

Perhaps the main motivation for educators to evaluate software stems from their concern about software quality. Evidence of this concern can be seen from two kinds of developments that have taken place since microcomputers began to be used in schools. First, educators have set up software clearinghouses to exchange information on the quality of software. Most of these clearinghouses conduct formal evaluations of software that are made widely available to other educators. Some of the clearinghouses that have done a large number of evaluations that can be accessed on-line with a computer and modem include Educational Products Information Exchange (EPIE), MicroSIFT, and the York University Faculty of Education On-line Service. In addition, regular printed evaluations are provided by publications such as *Software Reports* and the *Digest of Software Reviews*. There has been no other kind of teaching and learning resource in the history of education that has prompted such widespread efforts at evaluation. Second, educators have quickly become disenchanted with the quality of commercially available software, so they have begun forming groups to develop their own products. The best known of these are CONDUIT and the Minnesota Educational Computing Corporation (MECC). Again, these efforts are without precedence in size and scope in the development of educational materials.

Surveys of the quality of software have also shown that the overall level is low. Several software clearinghouses that have studied the issue have come to this conclusion independently. EPIE has on several occasions reported that only about five percent of the software on the market can be rated as "exemplary" ("Research indicates stalled software evolution" and "California sets software guidelines"); Alberta Education (1985, 1986) found that it could recommend fewer than ten percent of available educational software for adoption in schools in their jurisdiction; and York University has reported that only five to nine percent of the software titles it has evaluated could be considered acceptable (Owston, 1985b). In a study done at Columbia University Teacher's College of all evaluations carried out by EPIE, it was concluded that most software being developed is poorly designed and does not take advantage of the potential or capabilities of the microcomputer (Bialo and Erikson, 1985). Popular wisdom may suggest that the quality of software is improving; however, another study done by EPIE suggests that this is not the case ("What's in the educational software pool?"). An analysis of EPIE and non-EPIE evaluations conducted between 1980 and 1984 led EPIE to conclude that the overall level of quality of educational software had "stalled out" at the lower end of EPIE's "recommended with reservations" rating range during the last two years of the study.

From this discussion, we can see that educators are in the unenviable position of having to select software from a rapidly-expanding pool that appears to be maintaining a constant, low level of quality. Undoubtedly, there are software products available that far surpass the quality of earlier products. But the fact remains that this software makes up only a small proportion of what's available on today's market. Our mission then is to identify these superior products and let others know about them.

Previewing Software

Another reason to evaluate software is because it is very often difficult to get preview copies of software from producers. Therefore, reading evaluations done by other teachers will help you to make informed decisions because you may be forced to buy software sight unseen.

Educators are not used to buying teaching resources without being able to see them first. Book publishers have long recognized that the best way to sell their books is to let teachers have examination copies. Software producers, however, are reluctant to make preview copies available because they fear that the software will be illegally copied. Whereas the cost advantage and convenience of copying books are usually not large, they are significant for software. Software that is worth several hundred dollars can be copied easily for the cost of blank diskette; clearly, producers are looking for ways to protect their investment. But slowly, more and more software producers are realizing that to serve the educational community properly they must make preview copies of their software available. Policies vary from making products available for a 30-day examination to providing low cost or free demonstration diskettes. Some producers have even set up preview centers for teachers as an alternative solution. But until such time as policies like these become the norm for the software industry, evaluation will play a very valuable role.

Volume of Software

Even if preview copies of software become more available to educators, the sheer volume of software makes evaluation almost essential. An estimated 8000 to 10,000 educational software titles are now on the market, with about 2000 new titles appearing each year. Evaluation provides a means of sifting through the large numbers of titles to identify a manageable number for closer inspection.

Let's say you were looking for several titles that could be used for primary school language arts and you would be willing to preview about ten to make your final selections. If you searched any of the larger on-line databases you would probably be able to locate, without much trouble, about a hundred titles that might satisfy some very minimal criteria, such as microcomputer type and maximum cost. From then on, the task of reducing the number of titles from which to choose is more difficult. Simply reading descriptive information alone might help you narrow your choices by half. How would you narrow your choices further? At this point, if you were able to read evaluations of the remaining 50 or so titles, you would likely feel more confident in your selection of the final ten to preview. In this way evaluation plays a key role in isolating a manageable number of software titles for detailed consideration.

Cost of Software

Commercially available software typically ranges in cost from just under $50 for an instructional package for a narrow skill area or for an educational game to several hundred dollars for multi-level instructional packages and more sophisticated software tools such as word processors and spreadsheet programs. Therefore, before you make a decision to purchase software, you want to be able to gather as much information as practicable, including evaluations. If you don't, you increase the chances of making a costly mistake since the software probably won't be returnable.

Evaluation as a Discipline

Unfortunately, software evaluation has, in the past, been viewed in a limited way, with little regard given to the many years of effort that have gone into the development of evaluation as a discipline. Software evaluation should be seen as part of the much larger field of educational evaluation, along with course evaluation, curriculum evaluation, and school evaluation. If we take this perspective, we have much to learn from the discipline that will help us evaluate software.

Evaluating Educational Objectives

Let's say you were asked to evaluate some software designed to teach the addition of two two-digit numbers. How would you go about doing it? Most likely you would set out to determine if the program accomplishes its intended objective, namely the addition of two two-digit numbers. If you did this you would be drawing upon an evaluation model that has dominated educational evaluation for half a century. The educational objectives model was first proposed by Ralph Tyler in the *Eight Year Study*. Tyler, charged with the task of determining the effectiveness of the so-called "progressive" education programs in American high schools in the 1930s, reasoned that if the program's objectives are clearly specified, the program's effectiveness can be judged by seeing if students in the program attain the stated objectives. While this reasoning is almost self-evident today, at the time it marked a significant breakthrough in educational thinking. Indeed, it marked the beginning of program evaluation as a distinct field of study. Before this time, the terms *measurement* and *evaluation* were used interchangeably, if the latter was used at all. Earlier evaluation efforts were concerned with measuring individual differences among students. It did not seem to occur to early researchers that programs could be evaluated in any other way than by focusing on the individual. The educational objectives model, by contrast, allows the evaluator to use measurement as one of several possible strategies to study programs systematically.

Implicit in the educational objectives model are several beliefs. First is the belief that all of the program's objectives can be spelled out, and that a consensus can be reached on which are the most important for study. In our case of a simple piece of computer software designed to teach a very limited skill, this is not a problem. But as the complexity of the program to be evaluated grows, this assumption becomes increasingly difficult to maintain. Second is the belief that the program's objectives can, in fact, be clearly stated so that they can be measured. Tyler urged that objectives be stated in behavioral terms. In other words, they should be stated so that changes in student behavior can be observed at the completion of the program. Some educators have found this belief difficult to accept. They maintain that not all or even the most important outcomes of a program can be stated in behavioral terms. Other kinds of valuable learning take place that are not necessarily manifested by changes in student behavior. Such examples include changes in attitudes and the development of complex cognitive strategies.

If you did use Tyler's educational objectives model to evaluate the software we talked about, you might face some problems. First, you would have to set some kind of standard which, if attained by the software users, demonstrated the effectiveness of the product. If the users met the standard, you would probably be satisfied that the software was effective. What would happen, though, if the users did not meet the standard? What could you then say about the software's effectiveness? Unfortunately, in this case, you would find it difficult to interpret the results in a meaningful way.

Another problem you would face, even if the objectives of the software were attained, would be that the educational objectives model does not provide any guidelines for evaluating the actual worth of the objectives. Tyler did make reference to evaluating objectives in his monograph, *Basic Principles of Curriculum and Instruction* (Tyler, 1949), by saying that they should be passed through "screens" where they would be examined, but he did not elaborate on the nature of the screens. Clearly, some kind of assessment of the objectives is necessary. For instance, you might need to know if the software's objectives have any educational value, if the objectives are too fragmented, if the objectives are such that they can be mastered out of context of the program, if they match the curriculum you are following, and so on.

A third problem with the objectives model is that if you focus only on the objectives, you may overlook other unintended, valuable outcomes. In the case of the software we were looking at, you may find that its instructional approach, excites (or bores) users leading, in turn, to changed attitudes towards the subject. Or, you may find that the software does not teach the stated objectives but, nevertheless, encourages valuable problem solving discussion by its users.

Despite criticisms of the educational objectives model, many educators find the model appealing. It makes sense, and its principles are relatively easy to understand and to implement. Even so, attempts have been made to refine Tyler's thinking and to improve his model. The countenance model developed by Robert Stake (1967) is one such attempt. In this model, Stake provided for a means of taking into account the context in which the evaluation is being conducted, and he required that the objectives themselves be justified. Perhaps more importantly, Stake stated that evaluation must involve both description and judgement—the two countenances. Previously, the evaluator's role was considered to be one of description—collecting the data and presenting the results. Stake said that, moreover, the evaluator should interpret the data by explaining discrepancies between ideal and observed performance.

Beyond Educational Objectives

It was really not until the publication of Lee J. Cronbach's article, "Course improvement through evaluation," in 1963 that evaluators considered organizing their evaluations around factors other than educational objectives. Cronbach suggested that evaluators account for the decision-makers who would be reading the evaluation report and the kinds of information they would need to make their decisions. Applied to software evaluation, Cronbach's ideas would then cause you to ask, who is going to be reading my evaluation report and for what purposes will they be reading it? Will it be other teachers in my school who want to see if the software would be suitable to use in the classroom? Will it be my subject coordinator who must decide whether the software is worth purchasing for the school district? Once you have addressed these issues, you can collect the necessary kinds of data to answer these questions.

Once a break was made with thinking of evaluation as the process of determining whether educational objectives were achieved, many other models emerged. For example, Stufflebeam (1973) saw evaluation as the process of "delineating, obtaining, and providing useful information for judging decision alternatives," thereby setting out the actual steps of the evaluation process. In his model he specified the kinds of settings in which decisions are made, the types of decisions that are made, and the categories of data that are to be collected. Another approach is the utilization-focused model of Patton (1978) which emphasizes how the evaluation findings will be used. With this model it is first necessary to identify the decision-makers who will be using the evaluation report, and then to find out what questions they need answered to make their decisions. A major assumption made with Patton's model is that, by involving decision-makers in the evaluation planning process, the likelihood of the evaluation findings being used is increased.

Other evaluation models have also emerged that do not necessarily focus on the decision-maker or on objectives. One model of interest is the goal-free model of Scriven (1973). Rejecting the principles of the educational objectives model, Scriven maintains that knowing the objectives in advance of the evaluation can bias or prejudice the evaluator. Scriven urges evaluators to conduct their evaluations without looking at the objectives so that they will be able to observe both the *intended and unintended* effects. If you were using this approach to evaluate the software in our example, you would look at the actual outcomes of software use and compare them with those that you would determine in advance to be desirable.

The illuminative model used by Parlett and Hamilton (1977) offers a different framework for organizing an evaluation. In this model the evaluator describes what it is actually like to participate in the school or course being evaluated. If the approach were applied to evaluating software, you would be asked to describe your experiences in learning to use the software, the context or setting in which it was used, what you learned from using it, and what you consider to be its significant features.

In any school, course, or curriculum being evaluated there are typically several groups of people whose "investment" will be affected by the outcome of an evaluation. Their investment, or stake, may be a moral commitment to the object being evaluated, a direct involvement in it, or a financial commitment. Therefore, the success of the evaluation report may well hinge upon the acceptance of the report by these groups. The stakeholder evaluation approach suggested by Byrk (1983) recognizes this fact, and focuses on negotiating with the stakeholders the kinds of information the evaluation report will contain before any data are collected. Once all stakeholders have clear expectations about the report, they are more likely to make use of it. This model would be appropriate if the software you were evaluating was already in use by colleagues who held strong opinions either for or against it, or if the software developer was directly involved in the evaluation. In this case, you would want to discuss with these stakeholders their expectations of the report, and agree upon the kinds of information the report would contain before you began the evaluation.

The responsive evaluation model suggested by Guba and Lincoln (1981) is another model that uses a different organizer—the concerns and issues of the evaluation reader or audience. They suggest that the major purpose of evaluation is to respond to the information requirements of the evaluation audience, *i.e.*, their wants and needs. The model can be thought of as subsuming other evaluation models. For example, if the audience needs information on the attainment of educational objectives, that would be acceptable under the model. Or if the audience needs to influence decision-makers, the evaluation could be organized to provide that kind of information. The key to this model is identifying audience needs and responding to them.

Evaluation Principles

From this brief look at the broader field of evaluation, we can extract some general principles to help us evaluate software.

First, we can see that we need to look not only at the educational objectives of the software package we are evaluating. In fact, we saw that stated objectives can mislead the evaluator. We should look at both the intended and unintended effects of the software. Going back to our earlier example, we should be concerned with not only whether the software teaches the addition of two numbers, but how the software might affect students' attitudes toward mathematics, how groups of students might interact when using the software, and so on.

We have also learned that the evaluation can be organized around factors other than educational objectives. We might look at the kinds of decisions that are going to be made on the basis of the evaluation. Is the school considering buying the software? How important is the price in this decision? What are the advantages of one title over other titles? These are some questions the evaluation could ask to help the decision-maker. Or we might organize the evaluation so that the chances of the report being acted upon are high. To do this we would have to ask, who is likely to be reading the report? What kinds of information do they require? What kinds of decisions are they going to be making? We might organize the evaluation by identifying those individuals who have a vested interest in the evaluation and then finding out what kinds of information they expect to get from the report. Or by identifying the likely users of the report, and asking them what issues and concerns they have about the software. The evaluation can then be organized around their information needs.

A conclusion that can be drawn from our discussion of evaluation is that you, the software evaluator, must try to identify who is going to be reading or using the evaluation reports. Once this is done you should find out what kinds of information the readers need and why they need it. You should then try to collect information that will satisfy these needs and present that information in your report. Perhaps the ultimate test of the effectiveness of your evaluation is how well you satisfy the information needs of your readers. There is little sense in evaluating software unless you are aware of what your reader needs to learn.

Chapter 2 Existing Software Evaluation Approaches

Now that we have seen some of the reasons why we need to evaluate software and we have looked at the evaluation process in general, let's see what approaches are being used for evaluating software. We will first get an overview of the approaches that have been taken and look at several of these in detail. This overview will be followed by a discussion of some limitations of these approaches.

An Overview

Over the past few years the number of different approaches developed by educators has greatly increased. A search of the software evaluation literature would easily turn up 40 or 50 different approaches. The approaches seem to be distinguished by two factors:

1. *Formality*. The approaches vary considerably in their formality. Some advocate formal training for the evaluators, have organized networks of evaluators (usually classroom teachers), and on-going evaluation programs (typically supported by government grants or agencies, non-profit organizations, or universities). On the other hand, some approaches are distinctly informal. These tend to be designed for the individual classroom teacher. Frequently they include evaluation checklists that are freely circulated and easily used by the teacher without formal training. The

checklists are written by national or local teacher organizations, school board personnel, or individual teachers.

2. *Intended Audience.* The approaches also vary considerably in the breadth of their intended audience. Some approaches are designed solely for personal use by the evaluator, while others are disseminated widely through formal publications, on-line databases, or microfiche. Between these two extremes are other approaches intended for specific groups such as school boards or software developers.

These two factors, formality and audience, provide a convenient means of classifying software evaluation approaches. Figure 1 illustrates this classification scheme. We can see that there are four resulting categories of classification: formal/wide audience, formal/limited audience, informal/wide audience, and informal/limited audience. Now let's look at some evaluation approaches that are representative of each of these categories.

Formal/Wide Audience	Formal/Limited Audience
Informal/Wide Audience	Informal/Limited Audience

Figure 1: Categories of Evaluation Approaches

Formal/Wide Audience Evaluation Approaches

This category consists of the evaluation approaches used by national software clearinghouses. Common to each approach is an evaluation form or checklist that has been developed by the clearinghouse staff according to criteria they feel are important for evaluating educational software. The staff organize networks of teachers to conduct the evaluations and train them in their evaluation procedure. Some monitoring process is normally used to make sure that the evaluators are following the established procedures correctly. The evaluation results are then widely disseminated via print and electronic media. Two of these approaches are described next.

MicroSIFT

One of the first large and, perhaps, the most influential software evaluation projects to be undertaken is MicroSIFT, conducted by the Northwest Regional Educational Laboratory's Computer Technology Program. Until late 1985 the project was funded by the National Institute of Education, U.S. Department of Education. During this phase of the project over 500 software titles were evaluated. Now, with funding from the Office of Educational Research and Improvement, the focus of the project is on the production of quarterly evaluation reports that compare a range of software packages in a specific area, such as the use of databases in social studies. MicroSIFT's evaluations are disseminated through the RICE on-line database, which is accessed through Bibliographic Retrieval Services (BRS) in New York, through Education Resources Information Center (ERIC), and through various educational service agencies across the U.S.

The original evaluation procedure developed by MicroSIFT has four stages. Phase 1 consists of the "sifting" of software packages to sort out those suitable for evaluation. In Phase 2, the software that passed the first phase is described. This is usually done by MicroSIFT staff who complete a software description form which contains questions about the microcomputer configurations on which a package runs, instructional purposes, objectives, content, and documentation. At Phase 3 the software is sent to at least two teachers at selected sites in the MicroSIFT evaluation network. The teachers then complete a software evaluation form. Their answers may or may not be based on observation of student use of the software. The evaluation form has 21 statements about three software areas—content characteristics, instructional characteristics, and technical characteristics. Evaluators are asked to indicate their strength of agreement to each of the statements on a five-point scale. Evaluators also rate the overall quality of the software in each of the three main areas on a scale of 1 to 5, and select one of four options on the recommended use of the software. In addition, the evaluation form provides space for the evaluators to give written comments on the strengths and weaknesses of the software and any other relevant comments. Phase 4 was to involve in-depth observation of student use of software; however, this stage of the project was never fully implemented.

MicroSIFT no longer uses this model in its new thematic approach to evaluation but instead uses procedures and criteria developed specifically for the kind of software being studied. Nevertheless, the influence of the original procedure has been considerable. Although it was designed for participants in the project, many individual teachers, schools, and school boards have found the procedure valuable for doing their own evaluations. The International Council for Computers in Education (ICCE) publishes it under the title, *Evaluator's Guide for Microcomputer-Based Instructional Packages* (ICCE, 1984). The fact that MicroSIFT was one of the pioneers in microcomputer software evaluation, and that its evaluation guidelines have been readily available, help account for its influence on other software evaluation approaches and their widespread use.

Educational Products Information Exchange

Founded originally as a consumer information organization for educational materials, the EPIE Institute began evaluating microcomputer software in 1981 with the cooperation of Teachers College, Columbia University. EPIE has created a nationwide network of software evaluators, each of whom has been trained by EPIE staff. EPIE's operation has been supported by various non-profit foundations and subscriptions to its services and publications. Evaluators are "certified" by EPIE after successfully completing training and their work is monitored by other experienced evaluators. Their evaluations are disseminated in the publication, *Courseware PRO/FILES*, and on-line through Compuserve.

EPIE's evaluators complete a lengthy questionnaire that includes questions on software content, methods and approach, and user evaluation components. Questions are a mix of those requiring written answers of varying length, and those requiring a simple YES or NO answer. The evaluators are also asked to indicate on a four-point scale their extent of agreement to statements about the software's characteristics. EPIE's staff synthesize the evaluators' comments into 250-word reports. The reports also contain an overall recommendation on the suitability of the software.

Since EPIE closely controls the training and certification of its evaluators and does not publish its evaluation questionnaire, its approach is not as popular as MicroSIFT's. Still, EPIE's evaluations are widely read.

Formal/Limited Audience Evaluation Approaches

This category of evaluation approaches differs from the previous category because, although formal evaluation procedures are followed, the evaluations are targeted at specific groups and normally circulated only to their members. The evaluation approaches that would fall within this category include those that are carried out by state or provincial governments or local school boards. Evaluations done by group members who are trained by the host organization tend to be curriculum specific and, as such, are not likely to be as useful to broader audiences.

One of the major and most characteristic members of this category is the Alberta Education software clearinghouse. Alberta Education established its software clearinghouse in 1982 to provide guidance to provincial schools in the selection of software. Software that meets its criteria can be purchased by provincial schools at discounted prices through Alberta Education. Its evaluations are distributed semi-annually in printed reports. Although the Alberta clearinghouse is operated as a service to provincial schools, its reports are available to readers outside the province. Alberta Education warns these readers, however, that its evaluations should be read with caution since they are aimed specifically at the provincial curriculum.

Alberta Education has a three-stage evaluation process that uses trained classroom teachers. At the first stage, software is screened to eliminate inappropriate software from further consideration. Each software package that passes through the first stage is then given to a minimum of three teachers who have been trained in the use of the Alberta Education evaluation instrument. These teachers evaluate the software, with student input if possible. Unlike the evaluation instruments of MicroSIFT and EPIE, the Alberta instrument does not have any rating scales or short-answer questions. Instead, the instrument asks evaluators to supply narrative descriptions and evaluations of software in four areas—pedagogical content, instructional format, technical characteristics, and implementation support. Evaluators are given guidelines on what aspects of each of these four areas should be examined. After the Alberta Education staff synthesize the three reports, software that receives a positive evaluation is advanced to the third stage. At this stage the software is evaluated for congruency with the Alberta curriculum and is rated as a "basic," "recommended," or "supplementary" learning resource.

Informal/Limited Audience Evaluation Approaches

Included in this category is the large number of software evaluation checklists and forms that is developed for individual use by classroom teachers or groups of teachers. These checklists are often published in education journals or textbooks, or are developed locally to meet specific needs. Because they are intended for local use, the evaluations done with them are seldom circulated beyond the individuals or groups using them.

One of the better known evaluation approaches in this category is that of the National Council of Teachers of Mathematics (NCTM). The NCTM guidelines (Heck *et al.*, 1984) were developed for use by all educators in all subject areas interested in evaluating software, not just for mathematics teachers. NCTM suggests seven steps be followed when evaluating software, starting with familiarization, followed by testing the strengths and weaknesses of the software, observation of several students using it, completion of an evaluation checklist, and ending with a decision about using or buying the software. Central to. the NCTM approach is the evaluation checklist which contains descriptive and evaluative questions. The descriptive questions deal with basic information about the software including its uses and whether the software is designed for individual or group instruction. The evaluative questions ask teachers to indicate on a five-point scale their rating of the software on user orientation for students and themselves, content, features that motivate students, and the style in which instruction is provided. Evaluators are also asked to rate the effects of the software on the classroom social climate as "present and negative," "not present," or "present and positive."

Many schools and school boards have developed their own evaluation checklists that are used by individual teachers for themselves, their school, or school board. These would also be in this category, since the approaches are not part of a formal evaluation plan, and the evaluation reports are not widely disseminated. Frequently, the design of these checklists is heavily influenced by other published checklists such as NCTM's and MicroSIFT's.

Informal/Wide Audience Evaluation Approaches

The software reviews published in most education and computing periodicals such as *The Computing Teacher* fall into this category. Typically, the reviews are the opinion of one person who may or may not have used the software in the classroom. As in a book or film review, the reviewer begins by describing the features of the software, discusses its strengths and weaknesses, and then concludes with a recommendation. In most reviews, the reader does not know what guidelines or criteria, if any, the evaluator used, although some periodicals require that certain ones be followed. An excellent source for brief abstracts of reviews from a number of different sources, most of which would be in this category, is the *Digest of Software Reviews.*

Limitations of Current Approaches

Regardless of the category of software evaluation approach, all current approaches tend to be weak in at least four ways. These limitations will be discussed now because they point the direction to the development of the new evaluation procedure presented in the next chapter.

Comparative Nature

Current approaches tend to be comparative in nature. That is, evaluators are asked to rate software according to their strength of agreement to statements about the software, or they are asked to give written opinions on various aspects of the software. For example, one question in the MicroSIFT guidelines ask evaluators to say whether they "strongly agree," "agree," "disagree," or "strongly disagree" that the presentation of the software's content is clear and logical. Another example from the EPIE questionnaire asks evaluators to answer YES or NO to the question of whether the software is easy to run, and to give reasons for their answer.

Since none of the current approaches is based on explicit criteria, evaluators tend to judge software relative to other software they have seen. If the state of the art of software development were more advanced, there would be no problem because meaningful comparisons could be made. The absence of explicit criteria is a distinct limitation, though, when the norm is considered to be inadequate by most educators. Evaluators may respond to questions such as those above by saying, for example, "Yes, the software is easy to run." But what is meant by "easy to run"? Easier than software XYZ? The difficulty is that software XYZ may not easy to run and, even though a new piece of software is judged superior, it may still be inadequate.

Subjective Nature

Another problem is that current evaluation procedures tend to be subjective. This will not pose a problem if the evaluators are well-known authorities whose opinions are highly valued. A problem does occur, though, if the evaluators are unknown to the evaluation reader, which is most often the case in widely disseminated evaluations. We do not know what philosophy, beliefs, or biases the unknown evaluator is bringing to bear on the evaluation. Publications such as the *Digest of Software Reviews* help reduce this kind of problem because the reader can compare the abstracts of several reviews to look for trends or an emergent consensus. Nevertheless, the basic subjective element remains.

Poor Reliability

A problem stemming from the lack of standards and objectivity of current software evaluation is its inherent lack of reliability. Current approaches make little or no attempt to assure the reader that they have some measure of reliability, especially when two different evaluators rate the same software, or when the same evaluator rates different software packages.

Typically, evaluation consumers will be faced with the task of having to choose one software package from several that purportedly accomplish the same objectives. In the absence of any measure of consistency or reliability in the evaluation procedure, meaningful evaluative comparisons are very difficult to make. This limitation is even more pronounced when different evaluators evaluate different packages, than when one evaluator rates different packages.

Overall Impression

The difficulty of obtaining an overall impression of a piece of software is another problem with present evaluation approaches. These approaches often require the evaluator to answer as many as 40 or 50 questions about the software, yet provide little, if any, guidance in interpreting the discrete answers as a meaningful whole. Such guidance is necessary since, ultimately, the evaluation consumer is going to want to make an overall judgement about a particular package being considered. Those evaluation approaches that do offer some guidance suggest that the evaluator (or evaluation consumer) make a global rating by totalling the answers to individual questions in the evaluation instrument. For example, one procedure suggests that evaluators assign their own weightings to each individual question and then calculate a weighted total score. Another procedure suggests that the total number of YES and NO responses to an evaluation instrument be added to produce "the number of desirable characteristics in the program." Clearly, any such scheme is far too simplistic to take into account the complex interactions of the many important variables that combine to produce quality software. Yet without a meaningful overall impression, the reader is not able to make an effective comparison of similar kinds of software when making instructional or purchasing decisions.

Chapter 3 A New Approach to Software Evaluation

In the first chapter, we saw that three groups—classroom teachers, subject consultants and coordinators, and software producers—were the prime audiences for educational software evaluations. We also saw that the evaluation of software is important for educators because of:

1. the poor overall quality of commercial software;

2. the difficulty in gaining access to software for preview;

3. the sheer volume software which makes the selection of appropriate titles difficult;

4. the expense of software.

The limitations of present evaluation techniques include:

1. a lack of appropriate standard by which to judge software;

2. subjectiveness;

3. poor reliability;

4. the problem of forming an overall impression of the software. These problems suggest the need for improved evaluation procedures.

Clearly, any new evaluation procedure should build on the strengths of existing procedures, and minimize their weaknesses.

The evaluation approach described in this chapter was developed with this idea in mind. The approach is called panel evaluation. As the name suggests, panels of evaluators examine software according to specific procedures. The heart of the panel evaluation procedure is a criterion-based software evaluation scale know as the York Educational Software Evaluation Scales (YESES). In this chapter both the development of YESES and the panel evaluation procedure are described.

Development of YESES

Rationale

The rationale for the design of YESES was drawn from three sources. The first is the field of the assessment of student writing and, in particular, the analytical method of scoring writing (Diederich, 1974). In this field, it is assumed that there are several identifiable underlying traits of writing, all of which, in any context are considered important, upon which the writing can be judged. Furthermore, experts seldom have difficulty in agreeing on the nature of these traits, *e.g.*, organization, ideas, mechanics, wording. With the analytical method of scoring, a scale is developed for each of these important traits, and the writing is assessed by assigning a score for each trait. For instance, the "organization" scale might have four points. A paper receiving a rating of 4 would be one that is well-organized, logical, and on-topic. At the low end of the scale, a 1 might be a paper that is muddled, containing unclear and circular argumentation. Ratings of 3 and 2 would reflect varying degrees of organization between these two extremes. Crucial to the method is that the criteria for assigning the scores for each trait be explicit and thoroughly understood by the scorers. The analytical approach has been used successfully in classrooms by individual teachers and in large-scale assessment projects such as the National Assessment of Educational Progress.

The second field from which the rationale for YESES was drawn was criterion-referenced testing (Popham, 1978). According to this school of thought, the most meaningful method of measuring student achievement comes from determining the extent to which specific domains of knowledge have been mastered, rather than by comparing students with each other as is done in traditional norm-referenced testing. By doing so one can discover what the learner actually *knows*, instead of simply finding out that the learner knows more (or less) than other learners. Educators have found the concept of criterion-referenced tests appealing and the test scores easy to interpret, although the task of specifying the knowledge domains is sometimes very challenging.

The third area the YESES rationale is drawn from is the field of the assessment of oral proficiency in a second language. In particular, the rationale arises from the work pioneered by The Educational Testing Service on the U.S. Foreign Service Institute language examinations. Its methods were subsequently adopted by educational jurisdictions, the first of which was the New Brunswick Department of Education in Canada (NBDE, 1974). The assessment procedure requires interviewers to be trained and "calibrated" to a holistic proficiency scale. Through a structured conversation the interviewer is able to locate the overall proficiency of the interviewee at an appropriate point on the scale. The scale is interpreted by referring to sets of descriptors that set out in detail the language skills typical of an individual at that point. For example, the top point on the scale typically represents overall proficiency equivalent to that of a "native speaker," while the bottom point represents the ability to satisfy routine travel needs and minimum courtesy requirements in the second language. The technique has proven successful because it provides a reliable global assessment of a student's ability to communicate in the second language that can be easily interpreted by anyone who has read the assessment criteria.

Categories of YESES

A study of other software evaluation approaches, including those described in the last chapter, suggests that there are four distinct categories that educators consider important for the evaluation of drill and practice, tutorial, problem-solving, and simulation software. They are the pedagogical content, the instructional presentation, the documentation, and the technical characteristics of the software. For YESES, criterion-based scales were developed to evaluate each of these categories. Detailed definitions of the four categories are given in Appendix A. For this discussion the following brief definitions are sufficient:

Content   The skills and knowledge that the software
                    purports to teach, including their organiza-
                    tion, accuracy, and appropriateness.

Instruction   The manner in which the software takes ad-
                    vantage of the unique capabilities of the
                    microcomputer in conveying the content.

Documentation   The supporting materials and instructions,
                    available both in print and on screen, that ac-
                    company the software and explain its use.

Technical   The overall quality of the software design,
                    with respect to user inputs, software outputs,
                    and system errors.

A fifth category, Modelling, was offered for evaluating simulation software. While no other evaluation procedure uses this
category, it was included in YESES because simulation is an
extremely valuable kind of application for microcomputers in
the classroom. The addition of the simulation category should
help to encourage the development of quality software of this
kind. The category is defined as follows:

Modelling   The adequacy of the model used in the simu-
                    lation to simulate a real-life situation.

A detailed definition of this category also appears in Appendix
A.

Criteria for YESES

For each of the above categories a four-point criterion-based
scale was developed. Each point on the scales represents general
characteristics of software that would be rated at that level.
Level 4 represents "exemplary" software, level 3 "desirable"
software, level 2 "minimally acceptable" software, and level 1
"deficient" software.

The development of the descriptions at each level of YESES
was guided by an analysis of other commonly used software
evaluation procedures. This was done by making a list of all the
characteristics of software that would rate "high" and "low" on
the other procedures. The characteristics were then grouped according to the category of YESES that best described them.
Then the characteristics were summarized for each category,

giving "anchor points" for levels 4 and 1 of YESES. Descriptions of the two middle scale points, levels 3 and 2, were obtained by extrapolating from the descriptions of levels 4 and 1.

Detailed descriptions of each of the levels of YESES are in Appendix A. A summary of them follows:

Pedagogical Content Scale

> **Level 4: Exemplary**. Pedagogical content at level 4 is superior in its organization, accuracy, and appropriateness. The content is well-matched to the intended user's abilities and has a high educational value.

> **Level 3: Desirable**. The organization, accuracy, and appropriateness of level 3 content is not quite as favorable as that of level 4 due to relatively minor weaknesses. A few aspects of level 3 content might be of sightly questionable value.

> **Level 2: Minimally Acceptable**. Level 2 content is deficient in one area or a combination of the areas organization, accuracy, or appropriateness. The educational value of the content as a whole may be questionable.

> **Level 1: Deficient**. Content at level 1 is sufficiently substandard to call in to question the use of the software regardless of the strengths of its other characteristics.

Instructional Presentation Scale

> **Level 4: Exemplary**. Software at this level presents the content in a manner that takes maximum advantage of the unique capabilities of the microcomputer, allows the user to control the pace of instruction, and provides positive, supportive feedback.

> **Level 3: Desirable**. Software at this level of instruction still presents the content in a way that takes advantage of the uniqueness of the microcomputer; however, it does not accomplish this as effectively as level 4 software due to one or more minor weaknesses.

> **Level 2: Minimally Acceptable**. Level 2 software docs not make effective use of the unique features of the microcomputer due to one or more distinct weaknesses in the instruction.

Level 1: Deficient. Software at this level, the lowest on the scale, makes no attempt to use the unique features of the microcomputer to present the content or does so unsuccessfully. Often this level of software requires the microcomputer to function as little more than a "page-turning" device.

Documentation Scale

Level 4: Exemplary. Software at this level has clearly written, concise documentation that fully explains how the software may be used pedagogically and technically.

Level 3: Desirable. Level 3 software documentation, like that of level 4, describes and explains how the software may be used both pedagogically and technically; however, it contains minor pedagogical deficiencies.

Level 2: Minimally Acceptable. This level of documentation contains a minimal amount of usable pedagogical documentation, and the technical documentation may have some minor errors or omissions.

Level 1: Deficient. Documentation at this level is clearly inadequate to support the use of the software either technically, pedagogically or both.

Technical Adequacy Scale

Level 4: Exemplary. The technical adequacy of level 4 software is extremely high with respect to user inputs, software outputs, and lack of system errors.

Level 3: Desirable. This level of software is not as technically adequate as level 4 software owing to minor flaws in its design. The flaws, however, may be regarded as slight inconveniences, not serious enough to detract from efficient learning.

Level 2: Minimally Acceptable. Level 2 software has distinct weaknesses that are, at the very least, constant annoyances to the user and, at most, a detraction from efficient learning.

Level 1: Deficient. Level 1 software typically has flaws that hinder efficient learning regardless of the technical content and instructional presentation.

Modelling

> **Level 4: Exemplary**. Software at this level provides a highly realistic portrayal of a real-life situation, yet its complexity is within the grasp of the intended user.
>
> **Level 3: Desirable**. Level 3 software has a less adequate, though usable, simulation model.
>
> **Level 2: Minimally Acceptable**. The simulation model in level 2 software has some significant weaknesses, although the software is still usable in carefully controlled situations.
>
> **Level 1: Deficient**. Software rated level 1 on modelling is generally unusable regardless of its strengths in other areas.

When the full definitions of categories are combined with the full descriptions of levels, the complete version of YESES is obtained. This version of YESES is in Appendix A.

With YESES the evaluation process becomes one of determining which level in each category best characterizes the software being considered. In this sense the scale is criterion-based. That is, evaluators rate the software relative to pre-determined criteria. In this way YESES differs from software evaluation "checklists" which ask the evaluator to agree or disagree with a series of statements about the product.

Use of YESES

As mentioned earlier, YESES is a software evaluation instrument designed to be used alongside a process called "panel evaluation." The goal of panel evaluation is to arrive at a more holistic evaluation of educational software that is both meaningful to the intended audience of the evaluation and consistently reliable. The evaluation itself contains two components: ratings on four (or five) characteristics obtained from YESES and written summary comments by the evaluation panel.

Before the panel evaluation begins, a team of two or three evaluators should be assembled. Panel members might be classroom teachers having expertise in the content area of the software being evaluated. At least one panel member should also be familiar with the pedagogical use of microcomputers. If you don't have anyone else with whom to form a panel, you can still follow the panel evaluation process on your own. Unfortunately, you may miss some of the important insights that can occur when talking to colleagues about the software you are evaluating. Also, the evaluation may not be as reliable as it would be if you had worked with a group.

There are four main steps that are essential to the panel evaluation process. They are as follows:

Step 1: Study Evaluation Criteria

Study the definitions of each of the four (or five) key characteristics of the software together with the descriptors for each level of the scales of YESES in Appendix A. The sample evaluations given in Appendix C should be looked at carefully to give an idea of how YESES is interpreted.

Step 2: Familiarization

Become thoroughly familiar with the software being evaluated. First, read the software documentation and work through the software to get a general idea of how it flows. Second, emulate a very able student to test the limits of the software, its system of rewards or feedback for correct answers, and its branching capabilities. Finally, emulate a weak student to find out how the software handles errors. Again, note the feedback and branching capabilities.

If, during this step, racial, ethnic, or gender bias or stereotyping is found, discontinue the evaluation, skip to step 4, and indicate why the software does not warrant further evaluation. This procedure should also be done if the software contains programming errors serious enough to prevent it from operating as described in the documentation.

Step 3: Assign Ratings

Reach a consensus on the level of YESES that best describes the software in each category: Content, Instruction, Technical, and Documentation. If simulation software is being evaluated, it is given a rating on the

Modelling scale as well as the other four scales. You will note that there are no half-points on the scales of YESES—the software must be given a rating of either 1, 2, 3, or 4 for each category.

Undoubtedly, you will sometimes find that none of the scale levels perfectly describes the software being evaluated. Nevertheless, select the level which has the most features in common with, or is most similar in nature to, the software you have. A rule of thumb is that, if you are uncertain which of two adjacent levels on any scale to assign, choose the *lower* of the two. This procedure will prevent "inflation" of the scale ratings. Also, try to rate each characteristic independently, without allowing the rating on one characteristic to affect the rating on another.

Step 4: Write Evaluation Notes

After the software has been rated on all relevant scales, brief evaluation notes should be written on the panel's overall opinion of the software. Try to make these notes as constructive as possible. For example, wherever appropriate, point out ways in which the software could be improved, how it could be integrated into the curriculum, or what the implications might be if it were used in the classroom. Guidelines for preparing these notes are given in the next section.

After the evaluation is finished, it should be entered on an evaluation report form similar to the one in Appendix B. Readers of the evaluation report need to have descriptive information about the software as well as evaluative information. Therefore, the form includes space for entering:

1. the title;

2. the copyright date or version number;

3. the price;

4. the producer;

5. the various microcomputer configurations on which the software will run;

6. the school level for which the software is recommended;

7. a description of the main features of the software.

Usually, all of this information can be obtained from the producer's literature. If there are any inconsistencies between the producer's information and the panel's findings, these too should be pointed out in the evaluation notes in Step 4.

From time to time, you should give a software package evaluated by your panel to other panels of evaluators in order to compare your evaluations. This will help to ensure that your panel's use and interpretation of YESES is similar to others. A difference in opinion of one scale point on several of the scales is certainly no cause for alarm. But if you find that your panel is disagreeing with others by two or more points on several scales, you should probably go back and carefully study your ratings as well as those of the other panel. At the same time, review the level descriptions of YESES to clear up any misunderstandings.

Guidelines for Writing Evaluation Notes

Step 4 in the panel evaluation process requires that brief evaluation notes be written on the panel's overall opinion of the software. They are intended to supplement the scale ratings, not to restate the characteristics of the software conveyed by the ratings. In practice, evaluators often find the note-writing the most tedious part of the panel process. This is probably because the notes must be reasonably brief to give the reader a quick overview of the software, while providing sufficient detail to be of use. As an essential part of the evaluation, notes should be written as carefully as possible.

To help you write the notes, the following guidelines are offered:

1. Aim for notes to be about 150 to 200 words in length.

2. Write in complete sentences, preferably in the third person singular.

3. Be sensitive to sexism or sexual stereotyping in writing the notes. For example, don't refer to a teacher as "she" or to a student as "he" unless you actually mean it.

4. Avoid the use of technical terms or jargon that may not necessarily be understood by the readers of the evaluation report.

5. Make sure your written comments are consistent with the scale ratings. For example, if Content is rated 4 (exemplary), don't refer to the content in your notes as being of little or no educational value!

6. Explain any widely exceptional scale ratings. If all the scale ratings were 1, for example, except for one which was rated 4, give an explanation for the discrepancy. This is not to suggest that scale ratings cannot be diverse; rather, the evaluation reader may wonder why an otherwise "deficient" software package is so exceptional in one characteristic.

7. Avoid restating the criteria set forth in the scale ratings. The evaluation notes should give new, not second-hand, information to the reader.

Panel Evaluation

In this chapter we have looked at the essential elements of panel evaluation. Panel evaluation is a collaborative process. It involves groups of educators who work toward reaching a consensus on the overall value of a piece of software.

In summary, a panel must first become familiar with YESES, the evaluation instrument that is central to the entire process. YESES defines four key categories for the evaluation of drill and practice, tutorial, and problem solving software, and a fifth characteristic for simulation software. For each of these five categories there is a four-point rating scale. Each point on these scales has a set of descriptors giving general characteristics of software rated at that level.

After becoming familiar with YESES, a panel must carefully run through the software to learn how the software operates and how appropriate it would be for various kinds of learners. The panel must then determine which of the levels on the four or five scales of YESES best describe the software it is evaluating.

The final step in the evaluation is to write evaluative notes, giving the panel's overall impression of the software and other relevant comments. These qualitative notes, together with the quantitative scale ratings, offer a complete evaluation. The final evaluation report combines the complete evaluation with a description of the main features of the software.

Chapter 4 Conducting Panel Evaluations

In the last chapter we examined panel evaluation, a new approach to the evaluation of microcomputer software. Although panel evaluation was developed to improve upon other evaluation methods, it should not be seen as a replacement for other techniques. Clearly, there is no single evaluation approach that will suit the needs of all educators. Panel evaluation provides an alternative to educators who are concerned with some of the limitations of other approaches. What, then, can we expect from panel evaluation? What are some of the problems that we might experience when using the panel evaluation approach? These questions are the central issues that will be addressed in this final chapter.

What to Expect from Panel Evaluation?

Time

A common question new evaluators ask is, how much time is needed to do an evaluation? The answer to that, of course, depends on many factors such as the number of panel members, their similarity of views, their familiarity with the hardware, and the complexity of the software.

Generally speaking, an experienced panel whose members work together well as a team can complete an evaluation of simple drill and practice or tutorial software in about two hours. As the complexity of the software increases, so too does the time required to perform an evaluation. More complex simulation software, for instance, might take a full day to evaluate. Therefore, to be safe, plan on spending about 50 percent more time than an experienced panel if you are a novice evaluator.

Typical Ratings on YESES

New evaluators are often interested in typical ratings of software provided by the YESES scales. This valuable information allows new evaluators to get a sense of how liberally (or stringently) to interpret YESES.

Over 150 formal evaluations have been conducted at York University with YESES on a wide range of popular, commercially available software packages. Of the five scales of YESES, the Content scale and the Instruction scale typically endow the lowest ratings. The average rating on these scales is just over 2. Ninety-five percent of the software evaluated received ratings of either 1, 2, or 3 on these scales, with about an equal proportion receiving each rating. Only five percent of the software received a rating of 4 on the two scales.

The Documentation and Technical scales tend to generate higher ratings. Approximately 30 percent of the software was rated 1, 30 percent was rated 2, and 30 percent was rated 3; the remaining ten percent received ratings of 4.

Since fewer simulation software packages have been evaluated, average ratings for the Modelling scale do not provide a meaningful guide. Experience with the scale suggests that the ratings are, on average, higher than the other four scales, but still less than 3.

Reliability

Earlier it has been argued that consistency in the evaluation ratings from panel to panel is necessary if meaningful comparisons of software are to be made. How reliable, then, is the panel evaluation approach?

Observations suggest that the approach is reasonably reliable, indeed. On a number of occasions, sometimes months apart, different panels have evaluated the same piece of software. Usually when this has happened, panels have been in total agreement on the evaluation ratings with YESES. Occasionally, they have disagreed by one or two points on one, two, or three scales. Never have experienced panels disagreed on all four or five scales.

Comparison with Other Evaluations

Despite the limitations of other evaluation approaches, comparisons between them and the panel approach may be helpful. When a set of panel evaluations was compared with EPIE evaluations (Owston, 1985b), panel results agreed with EPIE results about two out of three times.

However, even when the panel evaluation and EPIE *agreed* on the overall quality of a software product, they did not necessarily criticize the same features. One evaluation questioned the manner in which a pedagogical approach was implemented, while the other was critical of the educational value of the software's content. In cases where there was broad *disagreement* about the overall quality of the package, the more negative review was likely to be as critical of the educational value of the activity as it was to be critical of the way in which the activity had been implemented. Usually it would not be critical of both.

Potential Problems

Lack of Panel Consensus

An important assumption of panel evaluation is that panels, through whatever means suitable, can reach a consensus on the ratings of a particular piece of software. The consensus serves as a check on the interpretation of YESES, which results in greater reliability in the final evaluation. There are occasions when panels cannot reach a consensus, however. While this does not occur often, panels should be prepared for it.

Several strategies can be used to deal with the problem of lack of panel consensus. One is to rate the software according to the majority opinion. The dissenting opinion should then be explained in the evaluation notes. This procedure, not unlike that used by court judges, is perhaps the fairest way of dealing with a minority opinion. It has been used successfully in the past, particularly when there have been disagreements over the educational value of software content. (An example of this procedure appears in the evaluation of *The Enchanted Forest,* Appendix C.)

Another way of handling a lack of consensus is to show the controversial software to an adjudicator who may be able to clear up the problem. An adjudicator might be a person who has had extensive experience in software evaluation or who is an expert in the field. If the dissension stems from a misinterpretation of YESES or a dispute over the accuracy of the content, the problem can usually be resolved and a consensus reached quite easily. This method is not likely to succeed, however, if the difference of opinion stems from opposing philosophical views of how learning takes place or from other deep-seated beliefs.

A third way to deal with a lack of consensus and perhaps the most radical way is to ask the dissenter or dissenters to prepare an entirely separate evaluation report. This is probably the best method of handling situations that cannot be resolved by the previous two methods. Readers of the evaluations will then have to decide between two points of view and base their decisions accordingly.

A final point should be made about panel consensus. While it may be more convenient for evaluation consumers to read a report that is a unanimous verdict, consumers may be able to increase their understanding of a piece of software even more by hearing different points of view. In fact, the general evaluation literature includes a model that allows arguments to be presented both for and against the program being evaluated, much as a court of law does. Furthermore, there should always be room for differences of opinion about the quality of software, as there is in other areas of education. The panel evaluation process might be viewed as a means of presenting differing opinions in the absence of a unanimous verdict. Therefore evaluators should not consider a lack of consensus to be a disaster, but an outcome resulting from the very process of evaluation.

Distinguishing between Scales of YESES

When evaluators first use YESES, they sometimes have trouble defining the application of its various scales. Evaluators may notice a problem with the software but not know which scale the problem affects. For example, if they detect faulty sequencing of a topic in some tutorial software, they may not know whether the defect should be reflected in the Content or Instruction scale rating. Or they may not know whether unclear directions appearing on the screen should be rated by the Instruction or Documentation scales.

Fortunately, this problem is not pervasive; analyses of YESES have shown that evaluators are, indeed, able to distinguish between the scales. Nevertheless, the best way to deal with the problem is to re-read the definitions of the scales and, if possible, to actually look at some of the software that has been evaluated in Appendix C. There is one rule of thumb that can help you distinguish between the Content and Instruction scales: Think of two teachers teaching the same topic. Although the teaching method varies with each instructor, the content remains the same. Content consists of the knowledge or skills taught, while Presentation describes the manner in which they are taught.

Evaluating Software Tools

Software tools, including databases, word processors, and spreadsheets, as well as other kinds of "open ended" software are being used more frequently in schools because they foster higher-order skills in students while taking advantage of microcomputer technology. Up to this point, we have been talking about the evaluation of drill and practice, tutorial, problem solving, and simulation software. Can the panel evaluation approach, in conjunction with YESES, be used to evaluate these other kinds of software? The answer is that YESES can be used for software tools provided (1) the tools have been developed specifically for classroom use, or (2) that it is clearly understood that generic tools evaluated for classroom use at a particular age or grade may be functioning outside their intended purpose.

When tools are evaluated, the Documentation and Technical scales are interpreted in the usual manner; however, the Content and Instruction scales need some further explanation. In this case, the Content scale should refer to the process the particular tool is designed to facilitate. Evaluators should consider the appropriateness of the tool for a given group of users and, in particular, they should focus on the complexity and educational value of the features of the tool. The Instruction scale, on the other hand, should refer to the software's capacity for taking advantage of the unique features of the microcomputer in presenting the tasks necessary for using the tool. Attention should be given to the provision of feedback (*e.g.*, in the case of user error), the extent to which the tool can be adapted to the users' needs, and the psychological climate created by the tool.

Bibliography

Alberta Education, *Computer Courseware Evaluations: January, 1983 to May, 1985.* Edmonton, Alberta: Alberta Education, 1985.

Alberta Education, *Computer Courseware Evaluations: June, 1985 to March, 1986.* Edmonton, Alberta: Alberta Education, 1986.

Bialo, E.R. and Erikson, L.B., "Microcomputer courseware: characteristics and design trends," *AEDS Journal,* 18, no. 4 (1985), 227-236.

Byrk, A.S., ed., *The Stakeholder Approach to Evaluation: Origins and Promise.* San Francisco, CA: Jossey-Bass, 1983.

"California sets software guidelines," *MICROgram* (December/January, 1984/5), 2.

Cronbach, L.J., "Course improvement through evaluation," *Teachers College Record,* 64 (1963), 672-683.

Diederich, P.B., *Measuring Growth in English.* Urbana, IL: National Council of Teachers of English, 1974.

Digest of Software Reviews: Education (all issues). Fresno, CA: School and Home Courseware.

Educational Products Information Exchange, *The Educational Software Selector.* Water Mill, NY: Educational Products Information Exchange, 1985.

Guba, E.G. and Lincoln, Y.S., *Effective Evaluation.* San Francisco, CA: Jossey-Bass, 1981.

Heck, W.P., Johnson, J., Kamsky, R.J., and Dennis, D., *Guidelines for Evaluating Computerized Instructional Materials.* Reston, VA: National Council of Teachers of Mathematics, 1984.

International Council for Computers in Education, *Evaluator's Guide for Microcomputer-based Instructional packages.* Eugene, OR: University of Oregon, 1984.

"Microcomputer courseware evaluation form." Water Mill, NY: Educational Products Information Exchange, 1985.

Micro-courseware PRO/FILES (all issues). Water Mill, NY: Educational Products Information Exchange.

New Brunswick Department of Education, *Manual for Interviewers of French.* Princeton, NJ: The Educational Testing Service, 1974.

Owston, R.D., *The York Educational Software Evaluation Scales.* York/IBM Cooperative Project Document 2. North York, Ont.: York University, Faculty of Education, 1985a.

Owston, R.D., *Software Evaluation Using YESES.* Paper presented at the annual conference of the Ontario Educational Research Council, Toronto, Ont., December, 1985b.

Owston, R.D., *A Criterion-based Approach to Software Evaluation.* Paper presented at the annual meeting of the American Educational Research Association, San Francisco, CA, April, 1986.

Parlett, M. and Hamilton, D., "Evaluation as illumination: a new approach to the study of innovatory programmes," in *Beyond the Numbers Game*, eds. D. Hamilton, B. McDonald, C. King, D. Jenkins, and M. Parlett. London, England: Macmillan, 1977.

Patton, M.Q., *Utilization-focused Evaluation.* Beverly Hills, CA: Sage, 1978.

Popham, W.J., *Criterion-referenced Measurement.* Englewood Cliffs, NJ: Prentice-Hall, 1978.

"Research indicates stalled software evolution," *MICROgram* (October, 1984), 3-6.

Scriven, M., "Goal-free evaluation," in *School Evaluation: The Politics and Process,* ed. E.R. House. Berkley, CA: McCutchan, 1973.

Software Reports (all issues). San Diego, CA: Trade Service Publications.

Stake, R.E., "The countenance of educational evaluation," *Teachers College Record,* 68 (1967), 523-540.

Stufflebeam, D.L., "An introduction to the PDK book *Educational Evaluation and Decision-making,*" in *Educational Evaluation Theory and Practice,* eds. B.R. Worthen and J.R. Saunders. Belmont, CA: Wadsworth, 1973.

Tyler, R.W., *Basic Principles of Curriculum and Instruction.* Chicago, IL: University of Chicago Press, 1949.

"What's in the educational software pool?" *MICROgram* (April/May/June, 1985), 1-4.

Appendixes

Appendix A. York Educational Software Evaluation Scales

Pedagogical Content Scale

Definition

Content refers to the knowledge and skills the software purports to teach—the organization, accuracy, and appropriateness of the material. **Content organization** refers to the sequencing of the knowledge and skills within the lesson or lessons, the breadth or scope of the skills and knowledge, and the depth of instruction or amount of practice given to a topic. **Accuracy** is concerned with the truthfulness of the knowledge and skills presented. **Appropriateness** deals with the suitability of the content for the intended user, including such factors as readability, the relationship between the complexity of the content and the intended user's ability to master it, and the educational value of the content *i.e.*, whether the time spent learning the content is justified because of its inherent value. If one or all of these elements—organization, accuracy, and appropriateness—are weak, the content may be judged less than exemplary.

LEVEL 4: Exemplary content

Level 4 content is superior in its organization, accuracy, and appropriateness. The content organization is such that the scope of the knowledge and skills is congruent with the user's ability to master them, the sequencing is logical and follows good pedagogical practice (*e.g.*, less abstract ideas are presented before more abstract ideas), and the depth of instruction is sufficient to give the user adequate practice before proceeding to the next topic. The accuracy of level 4 content is extremely high. Furthermore, the content at this level is very readable, well-matched to the intended user's ability to master it, and has high educational value.

LEVEL 3: Desirable content

The organization, accuracy, and/or appropriateness of level 3 content is not quite as favorable as that of level 4 due to relatively minor weaknesses. The organization may be weak because the content scope does not quite match the user's ability to master it; the sequencing may be illogical or not in keeping with accepted pedagogical practice; the intensity of instruction may be either slightly more or less than necessary, requiring the user to complete too many or too few exercises; and the user may not receive sufficient practice with the material before moving on to the next topic. Problems with accuracy might consist of questionable (but not incorrect) facts or applications of concepts. Level 3 content may also present some vocabulary or sentence structures that give intended users difficulty. Its material may be too complex or too easy for the intended user to digest, and some aspects of the content may be of questionable educational value. However, all flaws in level 3 content are slight.

LEVEL 2: Minimally acceptable content

Level 2 content is weak in either one area or a combination of the areas of organization, accuracy, or appropriateness. The deficiency, however, is not serious enough to prevent the use of the software, if no other better software is available, and if the instructor is able to rectify the deficiency. In its organization level 2 software may present too much material; it may be poorly arranged in sequence or not consistent with good educational practice; its instructional depth may be exaggerated or insufficient. Accuracy problems encountered with level 2 content include incorrect minor facts or applications of concepts. At this level vocabulary and content structure may be too difficult for the intended user, the knowledge and skills too difficult to master (or too easy), or the educational value of the overall content questionable.

LEVEL 1: Deficient content

Content at level 1 is sufficiently substandard to call into question the use of the software, regardless of the strengths of its other characteristics. Organizational problems may include weak, illogical sequencing, and content scope and/or depth of instruction poorly matched with the user's ability. This level of content may also contain factual inaccuracies or incorrect applications of concepts. The content reading level may be inappropriately matched with the user's ability, the knowledge and skills presented either too complex or simple, or the topics covered of dubious educational value.

Instructional Presentation Scale

Definition

Instruction refers to the manner in which the software takes advantage of the unique capabilities of the microcomputer in conveying the pedagogical content. Such capabilities include whether the microcomputer functions as an interactive learning device. Can it integrate text, graphics and sound into the learning experience? Does it offer immediate feedback on the user's mastery of the content? How well does it adapt to the user's needs? **Instruction** also refers to the psychological climate of the presentation—the control of the lesson as sensed by the user, the tone of the instruction, and the supportiveness of the feedback. **Instruction** is concerned neither with the quality of the screen displays nor with the sound quality.

LEVEL 4: Exemplary instructional presentation

Software at this level presents the content in a manner that takes maximum advantage of the unique capabilities of the microcomputer for which it was designed. Level 4 software has a format that involves extensive interaction; it integrates text, graphics, and sound wherever appropriate; immediate, positive feedback is given to the user, and it adapts to the user's needs by branching to an appropriate level of difficulty so that unnecessary routines do not have to be performed before the user proceeds to the next level of difficulty. With level 4 software, the user has a sense of being in control of the lesson—to progress, to review, and to exit at will. Moreover, the tone of the software's language of instruction and feedback is supportive and non-punitive.

LEVEL 3: Desirable instructional presentation

Software at this level of instruction still presents the content in a way that takes advantage of the uniqueness of the microcomputer; however, it does not perform this function as effectively as level 4 software, owing to such factors as minor weaknesses in the interactive capacity of the software; imperfect integration of graphics, sound, and text given the capabilities of the particular microcomputer; slow or non-constructive feedback or branching that does not adapt to the user's needs as effectively as possible. Other reasons why this software is not rated at level 4 might include less user-control over progress, ability to review or exit/re-enter at will, or a slightly inappropriate tone of the software language.

LEVEL 2: Minimally acceptable instructional presentation

Level 2 software generally does not make effective use of the unique features of the microcomputer as an instructional device. While some aspects of the instruction may be rated at level 3 or level 4, the overall quality of instruction can not be rated at level 3 because of one or more distinct weaknesses in the instruction. Typical weaknesses might include little or no attempt to integrate graphics, text, and sound; delayed or negative feedback to user responses, and little or no branching. In addition to having these weaknesses, the software may allow little control over the various aspects of its operation, and the tone of its language may be either indifferent or overly punitive.

LEVEL 1: Deficient instructional presentation

Software at this level, the lowest on the scale, exhibits no attempt—or an unsuccessful attempt—at making use of the unique features of the microcomputer to present the content. Often this level of software requires the microcomputer to function as little more than a "page turning" device. There may be no integration of graphics, sound, and text (if, indeed, the first two features are used); the feedback may be non-existent or inconsistent, rewarding incorrect responses more than correct responses, and users may have to follow a lock-step sequence to complete the lesson with this level of software. In addition, the software may not allow the user to have any control over its operation once the lesson has begun, and the tone of the language may be punitive or non-supportive.

Documentation Scale

Definition:

Documentation refers to the supporting materials and instructions that accompany the software, including the printed materials provided as well as the supporting information available on the screen. One purpose of the documentation is to describe and explain how the software may be used pedagogically, which usually involves giving information on how the software may be integrated into the curriculum, the objectives of the software, the pre-requisite skills necessary to use the software successfully, the age/grade/ability level recommended for the software, and suggestions and references for preparatory and follow-up activities. Another purpose of the documentation is to explain the technical use of the software, such as how to boot the disk, how to stop/start/re-enter the program, and how to access various program components. From a pedagogical point of view, both of these purposes must be served by the documentation.

LEVEL 4: Exemplary documentation

Software at this level has clearly written, concise documentation that explains fully how the software may be used pedagogically and technically. Level 4 documentation contains thorough information on how the software may be integrated into the teaching/learning process by providing complete information on pre-requisite skills and abilities, follow-up activities, worksheets where applicable, and bibliographic references. The documentation must also explain all aspects of the operation of the software including—but not limited to—how to boot the disk, stop/start/re-enter the program, use peripheral devices, and branch to components of the software so that the user does not have to spend needless time on trial and error. If the software can be used pedagogically and technically after a careful reading of the documentation, it may be rated at level 4.

LEVEL 3: Desirable documentation

Level 3 software documentation, like that of level 4, describes and explains how the software may be used both pedagogically and technically. Unlike level 4 documentation, however, level 3 documentation is not as helpful or specific in its suggestions on how the software may be integrated into the teaching/learning process. This may be due to minor omissions in some pedagogical aspects or to a lower overall standard in the pedagogical information. Normally, the technical documentation would be expected to be the same quality as level 4.

LEVEL 2: Minimally acceptable documentation

This level of documentation contains a minimal amount of usable pedagogical information and technical information with some minor errors or omissions. Typically, this level of documentation results in considerable teacher effort to integrate the software into the curriculum. Depending on their computer background, users may find that technical problems have to be resolved through trial and error.

LEVEL 1: Deficient documentation

Documentation at this level is inadequate to support the use of the software either technically, pedagogically, or both. Pedagogical documentation is non-existent or unusable at this level; technical documentation may be confusing, imprecise, incomplete, or a combination of all three.

Technical Adequacy Scale

Definition

Technical adequacy refers to the overall quality of the design of the software with respect to user inputs, software outputs, and system errors. More specifically, **adequacy of input** refers to the ease and simplicity of entering data into the computer. The **technical adequacy of outputs** refers to the aesthetic quality of the sound, graphics, and color, given the limitations of the machine for which the software was designed, as well as the clarity of the screen layout. **System errors** describes the ability of the software to continue to operate and not "lock up" regardless of the kinds of inputs the user enters.

LEVEL 4: Exemplary technical adequacy

The technical adequacy of level 4 software is extremely high. This level of software gives clear, precise cues and prompts so that the user knows when, and in what form, the input is required. Level 4 software avoids the use of characters with special meaning, requires a minimal amount of typing (unless the objective of the lesson is typing proficiency), does not distinguish between upper and lower case characters unless there is a pedagogical rationale to do so, accepts partial or abbreviated answers wherever appropriate (*e.g.*, Y for YES, N for NO), allows responses to be corrected before they are accepted by the machine, and restricts the input to the same location on the screen. The color, sound, and graphics of level 4 software are aesthetically pleasing, and the screen layout is uncluttered and consistent from screen to screen. Finally, level 4 software is of such technical quality that no system errors whatsoever are evident when software is in operation.

LEVEL 3: Desirable technical adequacy

This level of software is not as technically adequate as level 4 software due to minor flaws in its design. The flaws, however, may be regarded as slight inconveniences, not serious enough to detract from efficient learning. Initially, the user may be uncertain about some aspects of the input to the software, such as its form and location, but after some trial and error or reading of the accompanying documentation, the uncertainty should be cleared up. For example, the software may be occasionally inconsistent in accepting abbreviated responses or in the location of input. Other drawbacks of level 3 software may include color, sound, and graphics that are not as aesthetically pleasing as those of level 4, or a screen layout that is inconsistent or cluttered. Like level 4, level 3 software should not contain any system errors.

LEVEL 2: Minimally acceptable technical adequacy

Level 2 software has distinct weaknesses that are, at the very least, constant annoyances to the user and, at most, a detraction from efficient learning. Often this level of software demonstrates inconsistencies in the required form and location of its inputs. Unlike those of level 3 software, however, these inconsistencies are not always predictable and may require trial and error by the user to determine the form and/or location of the input. Examples of these inconsistencies include accepting abbreviations at one point during the lesson but not at another, distinguishing between upper and lower case letters sometimes but not always, and requiring user responses to be entered at different screen locations from one frame to the next. The color, graphics, and sound of level 2 software may be less than aesthetically pleasing and the screen layout may be cluttered. Although there may be no actual programming errors in level 2 software, the program operation could be improved.

LEVEL 1: Deficient technical adequacy

Level 1 software usually has technical flaws that hinder efficient learning regardless of the superiority of the content and instructional presentation. The form and location of the input may vary from frame to frame even more frequently and less predictably than they do in level 2 software. Poor color, graphics, sound, or cluttered and confusing screen layout may be other reasons why software is classified as level 1. Another reason may be that the software has programming errors that are detectable during normal operation.

Modelling Scale

Definition

Modelling refers to the adequacy of the model used in simulation software to simulate a real-life situation. At least three factors must be considered when judging the overall adequacy of the simulation model. First, the complexity of the model relative to the intended user must be examined. Most real-life situations are too complex to be modelled, even with a large number of variables; therefore, a balance must be struck between the realism of the model and the ability of the intended user to deal with all of the variables in the model. Second, all of the variables in the model must be relevant to the simulation. (For example, the relevance of the lunar cycle as a variable in a stock market simulation is highly questionable.) Third, the variables in a simulation model must interact and produce results similar to what would be expected in reality; otherwise the user might be misled. In short, to determine the adequacy of a simulation model, the evaluator must examine its **complexity** relative to the intended user, its **relevance**, and its **results**.

LEVEL 4: Exemplary modelling

Software at this level provides a faithful rendition of a real-life situation that is neither too complex nor too simple for the intended user. The variables included in the model are the most relevant ones to use for the given simulation. Furthermore, all of the variables in the model interact and produce results approximately as they would do in real life.

LEVEL 3: Desirable modelling

Level 3 software has a less adequate, though usable simulation model. The number of variables in the model may be too many or too few, rendering the model overly complex or simple. One or two of the variables may be slightly irrelevant to the model and replaceable by a more relevant variable or variables or eliminated. Moreover, the variables may interact in ways or produce results that differ sufficiently from reality to be slightly misleading, though not to the extent of rating the software at level 2.

LEVEL 2: Minimally acceptable modelling

Although the simulation model in level 2 software has some significant weaknesses, the software is still usable in certain contexts, for example, if the instructor thoroughly explained the weaknesses of the software and supplemented it with additional materials or experiences. One typical weakness of level 2 software is that the model contains too few or too many variables, making the software either too simple or too difficult for the intended user. Or the software may contain irrelevant or inappropriate variables that significantly decrease the quality of the simulation. A further difficulty with the model may be that the variables interact in ways or produce results that differ substantially from the real situation that is being simulated, to the point of misleading the user and causing confusion.

LEVEL 1: Deficient modelling

Software rated level 1 on modelling is generally unusable regardless of its strengths in other areas. The number of variables used in the model may fall far short or be in gross excess of what is appropriate for the intended user. Moreover, the variables included in the model may not provide a realistic simulation of a true-life situation. A final reason why the software may be rated at level 1 is that the variables interact in ways or produce results that are totally unrealistic or misleading.

Appendix B. Software Evaluation Report Form

EVALUATION REPORT FORM

NAME   _____

PRODUCER   _____

DATE/VERSION   _____

PRICE   _____

CONFIGURATION(S)   _____

LEVEL   _____

DESCRIPTION

_____

_____

_____

_____

_____

_____

_____

PANEL EVALUATION RESULTS

DATE OF EVALUATION _____

EQUIPMENT USED   _____

EVALUATORS   _____

RATINGS

     CONTENT   _____   INSTRUCTION _____

     DOCUMENTATION _____   TECHNICAL   _____

     MODELLING   _____

COMMENTS

_____

_____

_____

_____

_____

_____

_____

(Permission to reproduce this form is granted by the author.)

Appendix C. Sample Software Evaluations

NAME
THE ENCHANTED FOREST

PRODUCER
Sunburst

DATE
1984

PRICE
under $100

CONFIGURATIONS
IBM PC, color graphics card, color monitor and double-sided drive required, 128k
IBM PCjr, color graphics card, color monitor and double-sided drive required, 128k
APPLE II+, IIc, IIe, color monitor required, 64k
Tandy 1000, 256k

LEVEL
junior, intermediate, senior

DESCRIPTION
This program is designed to help students think logically and understand concepts of conjunction (and), disjunction (or), and negation (not). Students enter The Enchanted Forest to find strange-looking ponds that contain geometric shapes. An evil witch has turned all the animals of the forest into these shapes. To release the animals, students must learn (at the witch's school) to describe all the shapes in the ponds as sets involving conjunctions, disjunctions, and negations.

PANEL EVALUATION RESULTS

DATE OF EVALUATION
85/11/29

EQUIPMENT USED
IBM PCjr

RATINGS
CONTENT 2	**INSTRUCTION** 3
DOCUMENTATION 4	**TECHNICAL** 2

COMMENTS
The evaluators were in strong agreement about the quality of the documentation of The Enchanted Forest. However, there was some disagreement about the pedagogical content of this program. The publisher of The Enchanted Forest asserts that this program will promote logical thinking and problem-solving in children. It is assumed that presenting children with artificial problems will (or can) affect the development of children's logical thinking. One of the evaluators agreed with this conclusion. The other two evaluators doubted that isolated practice on skills presumed relative to logical thinking would, in fact, affect children's natural use of logical thinking and problem-solving. In fairness, this is an empirical question; the actual effect of programs such as The Enchanted Forest must be carefully researched. Until that has been done, the attraction of programs which attempt to teach problem-solving skills will depend on teachers' beliefs about learning. Those who favor a more holistic view of learning may be uncomfortable with programs like The Enchanted Forest which fragment learning. Teachers who believe that logical thinking can be isolated for drill may find The Enchanted Forest an attractive way to promote problem-solving.

NAME
HUMAN LIFE PROCESSES I - CELLULAR PHYSIOLOGY

PRODUCER
IBM Corporation

DATE
1985

PRICE
under $100

CONFIGURATIONS
IBM PC, PCjr, PC XT, PC AT

LEVEL
intermediate, senior

DESCRIPTION
This program explains some of the most vital processes of life: respiration, growth, regulation, synthesis, excretion, transport, nutrition and reproduction. It describes how even the tiniest organism goes through these everyday processes. Lessons cover the function and structure of plasma membrane, cellular respiration, oxidation and reduction, the role of ATP, and other physiological concepts. A quiz and test follow the lesson. An instructional guide is included.

PANEL EVALUATION RESULTS

DATE OF EVALUATION
86/02/28

EQUIPMENT USED
IBM PC

RATINGS

CONTENT 3		INSTRUCTION 4
DOCUMENTATION 3		TECHNICAL 4

COMMENTS
This program is designed for high school students, particularly those at the senior level in biology. Lessons could be used as an adjunct to classroom instruction or for independent study with

the appropriate pre-requisite background. Content is developed in a sequential manner and feedback is good though, in some instances, the program requires specific vocabulary in order for responses to be judged as correct. Information is presented in sequential steps by building new concepts based on previously acquired content. Animations and simulations help clarify and develop the concepts by maintaining student interest and inter-action. Students have control and easy access to the program through the use of a glossary and a Page Up/Page Down feature which allows for easy review and preview of materials. A Print Screen feature allows students to make copies of program screens. Documentation includes clear directions on how to op-erate the program and provides a summary of each section. Elaboration of suggested activities for classroom use (such as inclusion of recommended supplemental aids—charts, tables and diagrams) would facilitate the integration of the program.

NAME
ODD ONE OUT

PRODUCER
Sunburst

DATE
1985

PRICE
under $100

CONFIGURATIONS
APPLE II +, IIc, IIe, color monitor required, 48k
Commodore 64, color monitor required

LEVEL
primary, junior

DESCRIPTION
This program is designed to develop students' classification skills through five programs: Pictures, Words, Letters, Numbers, and Math Problems. Students are shown four items and asked to identify the "odd one out." The option of customizing the items, thus tying the activities to classroom materials, is also available. Varying levels of difficulty provide students with categorization problems. The program uses color graphics, animation and sound. Touch Window optional.

PANEL EVALUATION RESULTS

DATE OF EVALUATION
85/11/29

EQUIPMENT USED
APPLE IIe

RATINGS
CONTENT 1	INSTRUCTION 1
DOCUMENTATION 3	TECHNICAL 1

COMMENTS
Here is a favourite primary workbook activity which lends itself poorly to computer technology. Odd One Out has five different

programs: Pictures, Letters, Numbers, Words, and Math Problems. Children must find the item which does not belong within a four-square grid. Although the documentation provides worthy objectives and suggestions for classroom use, the software does not follow through. The examples that appear on the screen are too varied and possess little continuity. For example, Words, an exercise involving words associated with the Gettysburg Address, is followed by the study of suffixes and homonyms. Canadian teachers should be advised of some American content and spelling. There is, however, one feature that must not be overlooked. The Editor allows teachers to create their own programs to meet their students' needs. Although time-consuming, this function is worthwhile. The major drawback of Odd One Out lies in the technical area. Children must wait twenty seconds for their choice to appear on the screen. Frequent access to the disk may mean lost time and interest. One unusual feature is the use of a synthesizer voice to reward correct answers.

NAME
OPERATION: FROG

PRODUCER
Scholastic

DATE
1984

PRICE
under $100

CONFIGURATIONS
APPLE, 64k
Commodore 64

LEVEL
junior, intermediate

DESCRIPTION
The students learn about a frog through an on-screen dissection. They have a chance to investigate frog body systems repeatedly and at close range. Students can also work on putting the frog back together again. If they're successful, the frog will hop away.

PANEL EVALUATION RESULTS

DATE OF EVALUATION
85/11/29

EQUIPMENT USED
APPLE IIc

RATINGS
CONTENT 2		INSTRUCTION 2
DOCUMENTATION 3		TECHNICAL 2

COMMENTS
The basic activity of dissection and reconstruction of the frog and the accompanying reference material are suitable for students in the grades five to six level. However, the information presented about each organ is more appropriate for secondary level students, as far as concepts and language used. This in-

formation is presented without instruction or interaction. To be useful at this level, the program needs to provide activities which develop understanding of the higher-order concepts. The program could be improved further by increasing opportunities for learner/teacher control. Suggestions for program improvement: Allow students to select a particular organ as a starting point for study and provide a variety of operations related to the study of the organ; provide students with access to more information during their construction operation; provide more flexible and varied access to the dissection activity; structure more on-screen user help (*e.g.*, information about the "help" and "quit" commands). Conceptually, the program has a potential that is not realized in its current form.

NAME
PETS, LTD.

PRODUCER
MECC

DATE
1984

PRICE
under $100

CONFIGURATIONS
APPLE II, II +, IIc, IIe, APPLESOFT BASIC, DOS 3.3, 64k

LEVEL
junior, intermediate

DESCRIPTION
This package emphasizes the importance of responsible pet care. In Rhino students describe the resources they have available for a pet including living quarters, finances, and training time. This information is compared with the needs of animals listed in a databank. At the conclusion of the program, the students will receive a list of animals whose needs match the students' description. Pet Care provides a simulation of responsible pet ownership. Students are given the experience of caring for a pet by resolving typical events associated with pet ownership. To be successful, the students must care for a pet for the animal's normal lifetime. The program emphasizes the economic realities of maintaining a pet. A backup diskette and support manual is included.

PANEL EVALUATION RESULTS

DATE OF EVALUATION
85/11/29

EQUIPMENT USED
APPLE IIe

RATINGS
    CONTENT 2   INSTRUCTION 1
    DOCUMENTATION 2   TECHNICAL 2
    MODELLING 1

COMMENTS

The two programs in this package are intended to aid in the selection and care of pets. In spite of its stated purpose, Pets, Ltd., is a reading exercise with weak graphics, no sound, and a slow pace. The programs focus on the negative aspects of pet ownership and do not emphasize the positive aspects of affection and companionship which pets often provide. Because the information on pets is brief, and the pictures without detail or color, the child would probably gain more extensive information through book research. The junior level student would find the language level challenging enough but the content lacking in detail, interest, and relevance. The simulation program focuses entirely on the cost of owning a pet during its natural lifetime. The result is that the desire to own a pet is discouraged and the simulation of reality fails. The documentation does contain a minimum of useful activities; however, these tend to emphasize the recapitulation of on-screen summaries, resulting in a copying exercise. A print-out of the list of possible pets and related information might be useful. The program assumes that the child will use predetermined answers within established categories. It disregards input that does not conform to these anticipated answers. A more open-ended approach would be helpful. The programs present pets in a cold, calculating manner. A more humane approach is needed. Fewer full screens of text would make the program more interesting. Animation would help alleviate the rather dull presentation.

NAME
THE POND

PRODUCER
Sunburst

DATE
1984

PRICE
under $100

CONFIGURATIONS
IBM PC, color graphics card required, 64k
IBM PCjr, color graphics card required, 128k
APPLE II+, IIc, IIe, 48k
Commodore 64
TRS-80 color, 32k
Tandy 1000, 256k
Atari 400, 800, XL, 32k

LEVEL
primary, junior, intermediate, senior

DESCRIPTION
A small frog, lost in a pond of lily pads, helps students recognize and articulate patterns, generalize from raw data and think logically. The program has a practice option and a game option. The practice option allows the students to choose from six ponds, or levels of difficulty, in which lily pads are displayed in increasingly complex patterns. The students' task is to determine the pattern that will get a frog across the pond. The game option allows the student to collect points by directing the frog through as many ponds as possible, with the fewest number of moves. Emphasis is on efficiency of pattern.

PANEL EVALUATION RESULTS

DATE OF EVALUATION
85/11/29

EQUIPMENT USED
APPLE IIe

RATINGS
  CONTENT 3   **INSTRUCTION** 3
  DOCUMENTATION 4   **TECHNICAL** 3

COMMENTS

This program presents an upbeat and spontaneous approach to problem solving. By moving a frog from lily pad to lily pad, students find patterns and test their hypotheses. The truly unique feature of this software is that the child can build upon the strategies that were discovered at earlier stages. For this reason, it is important that the child proceed through the six levels of practice before attempting the games. The Pond is likely to encourage cooperation and interaction among children. The content is excellent but the sequencing appears illogical. Levels three and four (three-step patterns) were actually more difficult that levels five and six (four-step patterns). In the practice mode it would be beneficial to provide on-screen clues or positive feedback to help the child complete the task after several unsuccessful attempts. One attractive feature is an animated frog that splashes into the water and winks when he reaches the magic lily pad. However, there is some discrepancy between the number of jumps and the number of lily pads. It would help if the sound accompanied the landing of the frog on the lily pad. On a technical note, the space bar should be used to make selections instead of the arrow keys. The exemplary documentation includes well-defined objectives, learning strategies and practical suggestions for classroom applications.

NAME
SOLVING WORD PROBLEMS

PRODUCER
IBM Corp. and Test Master, Inc.

DATE
1985

PRICE
under $100

CONFIGURATIONS
IBM PC, PCjr, PC XT, PC AT

LEVEL
junior, intermediate

DESCRIPTION
This program presents math-related word problems such as figuring tax, discounts or averages and gives step-by-step instructions for their solution. This Private Tutor course not only allows students to progress at their own pace but also helps reinforce learning through a series of quizzes. This program requires Private Tutor version 2.00.

PANEL EVALUATION RESULTS

DATE OF EVALUATION
86/01/31

EQUIPMENT USED
IBM PC

RATINGS

CONTENT 2	INSTRUCTION 1
DOCUMENTATION 1	TECHNICAL 2

COMMENTS
This program has a number of serious limitations. The apparent purpose of this program is to provide instruction to students in solving word-problems. However, while students are drilled on these skills, actual instruction in analyzing and interpreting mathematical problems in context, *i.e.*, word problems, is not

provided. The difficulty level of the questions was generally below that which would be expected to challenge the average sixth-grader. The format of problems presented to students is also a concern. The multiple-choice format, including the correct response and three distractors, makes it possible for students to merely guess until they choose the correct answer. The number of attempts required by the students to select the correct response is not recorded—only whether or not the correct answer is chosen. The program may be more applicable to students in grades three to eight. Additionally, the documentation includes no guidance for teachers on how to integrate this program into the math curriculum. The ease of use of the program could be improved by providing instructions for moving forward/back and in/out of the lessons on the screen. However, this minor alteration would not compensate for the more serious limitations of this software in the areas of instruction and documentation.

NAME
STICKYBEAR ABC

PRODUCER
C.P.R. Software

DATE
1982

PRICE
under $100

CONFIGURATIONS
APPLE II, II +, IIe
Commodore 64

LEVEL
primary

DESCRIPTION
This is an alphabet program for young children. To operate the program the child simply presses a letter. When a letter such as A is pressed, an airplane is displayed on the screen. The program was designed to familiarize the child with the keyboard and to reinforce letter recognition. A book and a poster are included.

PANEL EVALUATION RESULTS

DATE OF EVALUATION
85/03/01

EQUIPMENT USED
APPLE IIe

RATINGS
CONTENT 2   INSTRUCTION 2
DOCUMENTATION 1   TECHNICAL 3

COMMENTS
The color, music and movement of cartoon-like pictures in this program would appeal to a pre-school child. The program is very easy to use, since the child need only push a selected letter key to change the picture. The task of letter selection is static

and one-dimensional in that there is no challenge either in the level of difficulty or the degree of control. Adult interaction would be required in order for young children to learn letter names from this program; however, a six-year-old child may be able to extend the demands of the program by making up simple games, using the letters, words and pictures which appear on the screen. The pictures on the accompanying poster match those in the program but the *Strawberry Look Book*, which is a part of the package, seems to be in no way related. The program could be improved by increasing the number of options for each letter, and by adding a voice component to reinforce the letter names.

NAME
STORY TREE

PRODUCER
Scholastic

DATE
1984

PRICE
under $100

CONFIGURATIONS
APPLE II, II+, IIe, IIc, 48K RAM, disk drive required; color monitor, printer optional
Commodore 64, disk drive required, color monitor, printer optional
IBM PC, IBM PCjr, 64K with DOS 1.1 or 128K RAM with DOS 2.0 or 2.1, color monitor, printer optional

LEVEL
junior, intermediate, senior

DESCRIPTION
This is a program for writing and reading interactive stories. An interactive story lets students make choices about the way the story unfolds. Stories branch out from one beginning to many different endings. With this program, students write page by page, linking plots in various ways.

PANEL EVALUATION RESULTS

DATE OF EVALUATION
85/06/07

EQUIPMENT USED
APPLE IIe

RATINGS
CONTENT 2	INSTRUCTION 3
DOCUMENTATION 3	TECHNICAL 3

COMMENTS

For students who are interested in a variation of story-writing and who are good writers, this program provides a challenging experience. The program is based upon the concept of writing stories which branch into various alternatives. In this way it makes effective use of the microcomputer. However, this type of story-writing, which requires mapping out of choices, represents a limited aspect of writing and could discourage inexperienced writers. In addition, the sequencing of activities within the program makes it difficult to become involved with the story-writing activity. The documentation is extensive and, if read thoroughly by the teacher or user, provides all the information and applications necessary for use of the program.

NAME
SUPERKEY

PRODUCER
Bytes of Learning/Scholastic

DATE
1985

PRICE
under $100

CONFIGURATIONS
APPLE II +, IIc, IIe

LEVEL
primary, junior, intermediate, senior

DESCRIPTION
This program is designed to teach basic keyboarding by touch. The program has four main parts: Posture introduces correct body and hand positions; Finger Names is designed to teach the terms which are used in the lessons and introduces the home row position; Lessons contains ten units which are designed to develop the students' keyboarding technique; and Skill Check provides practice, assesses progress, and suggests ways of improvement. A complete manual with special tips, ideas for teachers, and reproducible charts and record sheets is included.

PANEL EVALUATION RESULTS

DATE OF EVALUATION
85/11/29

EQUIPMENT USED
APPLE IIe

RATINGS
CONTENT 3		INSTRUCTION 3	
DOCUMENTATION 3		TECHNICAL 3	

COMMENTS
With a few minor program modifications this could become an exemplary piece of software. The program is designed to de-

velop keyboarding skills for both children and adults. The use of graphics makes each step clear, and the display keyboard matches whatever model of Apple computer is being used. The skills are developed in a logical sequence, allowing the students as much time and practice as necessary to master each skill. Clear prompts are given to guide the students through the program and to aid in correcting errors. Feedback is quick, positive, and accurate, and incorporates a variety of responses. The students move readily within the program and escape to the Menu at any time. Branching is used effectively to tailor the program to the individual needs of the learner. A backup disk is provided. In the initial lessons the terms "sentence" and "paragraph" are used when referring to random groups of words. Changing the terminology could eliminate the confusion. In the Skill Check section, frustration may occur when the students try to make a precise copy of the exercise by either using the Return Key to begin a new line, or filling spaces at the end of each line, using the Space Bar. Knowing in advance that this program has a wrap-around feature could alleviate this problem to some extent. If more than ten errors are made, no display of the errors is given. Perhaps if many errors are made, at least the first ten could be displayed to give the user some indication of where improvement is required. Many suggestions for integrated activities are given. One involves the use of a cardboard keyboard. Perhaps a full-sized, reproducible copy could be provided.